I Am Becoming:
God Delivered Me from Myself

Jade Thomas

Series: Book 1

Copyright © Jade Thomas

All rights reserved.

God Delivered Me from Myself is based on a true story. Some names and identifying details have been changed to protect the privacy of individuals.

Although the author and publisher have made every effort to ensure that the information in this book was correct at press time, the author and publisher do not assume and hereby disclaim any liability to any party for any loss, damage, or disruption caused by errors or omissions, whether such errors or omissions result from negligence, accident, or any other cause.

No part of this book may be reproduced, stored in a retrieval system, or transmitted in any form or by any means, electronic, mechanical, photocopying, recording, or otherwise, without the prior written permission of the author, except as provided by USA copyright law.

ISBN: 979-8-9887677-7-0

Printed in the United States of America

T. Fielding-Lowe Company, Publisher

https://www.tfieldinglowecompany.com

"God Delivered Me from Myself" is dedicated to every woman that's had the same experiences that I have. I want you to know that you can and will make it.

Jade

TABLE OF CONTENTS

Introduction..
How It All Started..1
Grade School..3
Losing My Virginity...5
Trying To Fit In...7
Too Much Sex Led To Abortions.........................9
High School Years...12
The Man of My Dreams.....................................14
My First Son..15
My Days In Prostitution.....................................17
Finding The Determination To Leave................20
Caretaker and a Loss..22
Yet Another Devastating Loss...........................24
The Abuse..27
He Left Me Broken..31
The Woman: Abomination.................................35
After Jesus Christ...38
God Saves My Life Again..................................40
The Struggle..42
The Temptations..43
Covid-19..44
The Loss of My Sister Chanel............................48
The Presence..52
Facing reality...53

God Supplies ALL of My Needs……………………………..…54
The Move……………………………………………………………55
Reviving……………………………………………...………………57
God Is Not Done With Me………………………………….……59
God's Promises To His Children………………………..……61
Jesus Still Loved Me…………………………………………..…63

INTRODUCTION

My name is Jade Norrel Thomas. First, I want to say how much of a privilege, honor, and blessing it is to write this book. I didn't think I would be around long enough to see the age of 30, never mind 39. At one point in my life, I hated myself that badly. It even got to where I didn't want to live anymore. Life wasn't great, and I felt I had nothing to live for. I didn't even know why God created me. I never fit in anywhere I went; I was always an outsider, an outcast. I felt like I wasn't good enough, didn't think I had any talents, didn't want to look at myself in the mirror, nor did I want to receive any positive feedback about myself. I didn't care how I lived my life. I was reckless and unmotivated to do anything. My mind was messed up in many ways.

It was never in me to share my life because of what I've been through. Who wanted to read about a woman that was depressed? Who wanted to read about an ex-prostitute who was unmotivated, didn't care who she slept with, and had no desire to do anything to improve her life? Who would care about a confused bi-sexual woman who had a few abortions, an abused single mother of three children who had so many men in and out of her life?

This book is not for everyone. This is a book that not a lot of people can stomach. Some may look at this book and find it disgusting, pitiful, pathetic, and outrageously degrading on all levels. If that is the case, this book is not for you. This book is for the ones who have experienced abuse, prostitution, and being a single mother. This book is for the mother trying so hard to care for her children, struggling with her self-esteem, and trying to overcome. I want them to know that there is another woman who has been through what they are currently going through. There is no judgment.

I am sharing my story to hopefully reach at least one woman. My life has been full of shame, embarrassment, harassment, alcohol, run-ins with the police, courthouses, prostitution, depression, oppression, setbacks, letdowns, mental anguish, death, and Resurrection. No one could survive what I have been through without the power of God. My life is not my own; my story does not belong to me. Sharing my story will be worth it if it can help save at least one person from going down or continuing down this road of destruction. I want you to know you deserve better than what you are going through. You are worth more. You deserve to know that there is a God who loves and cares for us.

1. How It All Started

I was born in Roxbury/Roslindale, Massachusetts. I was called "Wrong Way Jade" because I was a breech baby. As far back as I can remember, I had a very good life and all I needed at that age.

At the age of 7, my family wanted to leave Roxbury and move to a better location, so in 1990 my mother found a home in Brockton, Massachusetts. We were an average size family, my mom, my sister Chanel, my stepdad, and my two grandmothers. Looking back, I can say I had a pretty good life for a 7-year-old. I had so many material things but was missing the most important piece: love. It was depressing to wake up every day to see all the stuff I had and still feel lonely. I long for love.

I have always felt like I did not belong. That there was something different about me. I would not allow people to get close to me. If they did, the friendship would only last for a short time. The friends that I did have kept me at arm's length. They did not want to spend time with or invite me to events and gatherings, including my family. I was left out.

Was it the way I spoke? Was it the way I walked? Not being invited or supported in certain things, yes, it did hurt. I felt like there was something wrong with me. I knew I was different, but I felt we were all different in our own way. What exactly was it about me that I could not have friends? I was just like everyone else!?

2. Grade School

Going into the first grade in my new town, I was not welcomed as the new kid, which had many disadvantages. I wasn't allowed to sit at certain tables, nobody wanted to sit with the new girl, and I was considered an outcast. As days went by, things did get better and better. I was able to make some new friends. It wasn't long before I realized I didn't get along with other girls. There was always an issue, some jealousy, or they just didn't like me. I could have an attitude, yes, but at this point, I was trying to fit in.

After years of struggling to find my place in elementary school, I made it out of the 6th grade into middle school. I thought my life would improve, that I would make new friends and be happier, but I let my hope get the better of me. I questioned the loyalty of the friends I had. As much as I had an attitude, they did too, which is probably why we didn't get along being so similar. To make matters worse, as I entered the 7th grade, one of my legs became longer than the other. I got called Frankenstein because I was tall with a limp.

My teenage years were tough, lonely, and I was pretty much alone. I was not part of a clique; I was an outcast again. I was picked on for everything I said or did. I was not much of a talker because I had a secret that only my family knew. I had a stutter, and it was so embarrassing. I could not articulate the words that I wanted to say. I had so much to say that I felt people did not want to hear.

I felt like my own family made fun of me. I did not have a chance in the world. I never got the help I needed. I never got a speech therapist or any other support resources from school. So I went on living in fear of speaking. I never voiced my opinion and didn't wish to share my feelings, especially in public. No one asked about my feelings, and they probably didn't care.

3. Losing My Virginity

As I entered the 8th grade, my downward spiral began. I met a few girls that I thought were pretty cool. One of the girls and I started to hang out after school. Either I would go to her house, or she would come to mine. We did a lot of things together, and I thought I could confide in her. I was comfortable sharing some things with her, like family problems or school issues, but some were too deep, so I kept them to myself.

I was introduced to many guys that didn't go to the middle school I was in. At the time, I didn't think anything was wrong with that. One person in particular was a man named Shiz. We talked for a good while, mainly about the people we knew. Then things started to get a little heated between him and me as we began to talk about having sex. At the time, I was still a virgin and about 14 years old, while Shiz was 18. I was so attracted to him, and I thought he was attracted to me. Little did I know he only wanted to have sex with me, nothing more.

We arranged for him to come over to my house. My parents were on vacation, and my grandmother and great-grandmother were the only two at home. They lived on the first floor, and I was on the third. They couldn't hear anything, thank goodness. I was very scared because I didn't know what to expect, considering it was my first time. It was nothing like I had ever felt before. It hurt so bad, but it felt good. After everything was said and done, I noticed that I was bleeding. Immediately, I started to get scared. I didn't know what was happening to me, my body. Shiz explained that it was normal and that I was no longer a virgin. I didn't know how to feel about that.

I got on the phone with my friend and told her what had happened. She asked me so many questions. When I returned to school the following day, I experienced a shock I wasn't prepared for. I was told that I had slept with someone's boyfriend. Shiz had a girlfriend. I did not know that. People were so mad at me, wanting to jump me and everything else.

Shiz and I did talk one other time but never interacted much after that. I needed someone to speak with, so I told my guidance counselor what happened and wrote in my journal that I lost my virginity. Of course, my mother went through it. She was very upset. Once I told her how old Shiz was, she called the police. He was not happy as he could have gone to jail, but because it was consensual, there was nothing the police could do. My mother thought it would be a good idea for me to see a psychologist. She knew I was going down the wrong path.

4. Trying To Fit In

After all that happened, conversations started to come up about God with my mother and even more so with my great-grandmother, Evelyn. She was very wise and full of knowledge. She didn't want to hurt me but knew it was for my own good. I didn't want to hear anything about this God that people kept telling me about.

God was only brought up when I was in trouble, and I didn't hear about Him. I felt I was a typical 14-year-old girl. What was so bad about what I was doing that God had to be brought up? I didn't think I was doing anything wrong, I didn't think that it was affecting anyone, I wasn't bothering anyone. But in actuality I was causing so many problems in my home, even though my home had problems but I added to the problems that were going on in the home. The adults saw things I couldn't see, so they knew that God would have been the only that could have gotten ahold of me. Because of my stubbornness, me being hard headed, being disrespectful, disobedient, and the list goes on and on.

When I was in 8th grade, I thought I knew it all. As I explained to Shiz, I bit off more than I could chew, and things started to get extremely heated. I didn't think things would get so complicated. As far as having sex with these guys was going to be a problem, getting involved with these guys not knowing they had a girlfriend, but it wasn't like I wanted a relationship from them, just sex. My life was a hot mess; I couldn't go on without having sex. I didn't like the person I was becoming, but then, at the same, I loved the person I was becoming because I was getting the "love" I didn't think I would ever get from my dad. If only I had known God when people tried to push Him on me back then. At the time, I didn't want Him. I wasn't ready. I didn't believe in God. I didn't believe in His power, His love. Boy, was I wrong? If I had listened to my family when they pushed God on me, I firmly believe I would not have gone through what I went through.

5. Too Much Sex Led To Abortions

Ever since that one night with Shiz, I had wanted sex more and more. It was becoming a bit much. I was sure I wanted my life to be different. The only thing I knew I didn't want was to constantly be at my house, so I created reasons not to be there. I would leave my house in the middle of the night, ensuring I returned before my mother woke up. I wanted to do what other girls my age were doing at the time, not drugs or drinking, but being around my friends and not feeling like a prisoner in my own home.

I made a big mistake at the end of my 8th-grade year. Looking back on it, I'm grateful that I am still alive. My mistake was going to a guy's house when I knew several guys would be there. You might be wondering what I was thinking. I just wanted to have fun, but that fun immediately took a turn. That fun came with a cost.

Before I left that night, a few guys I didn't know approached me. They led me to the bedroom, where I sat on the bed. They held me down and had sex with me. What disturbed me most was the guys who did know me did nothing to help. By the time I got to school the next day, I was the center of attention and it was not good.

I was so embarrassed to have most of the 8th-grade class think of me in a derogatory way. A few days later, as I was hanging out with my so-called friends, I was told I was on another friend's hitlist. I wasn't sure what that meant, so someone explained that a guy wanted to kill me. I was so scared to go outside.

Going to that house brought me problems, and I had no one to blame but myself. The guy who wanted me dead could have done it many times over. He had seen me over and over at school. The consequences of my choices could have been great. God certainly had his hands on my life, no question about it.

How many times do we ignore God's love for us? I didn't realize then how much God loved me and why I wasn't supposed to die. I made many mistakes in my youth but rarely owned up to them. How many times do we blame our mistakes on our upbringing or the situation that we're in?

So many things were happening at that time in my life.. I was skipping school, making friends with drug dealers, continuing to have sex with multiple men whenever I could, and having abortions. I'm not proud of the decisions I made.

The abortions were hard emotionally, but I didn't realize at the time how it was even worse spiritually. I knew so many girls who had abortions then. It seemed normal. Being encouraged to have an abortion and realizing I was killing a child had a lasting, horrible impact on me.

6. High School Years

In my first couple of years in high school, I was trying to behave. My mother, at this point, was tired of my nonsense. As a 14-year-old, I had my own plans, which weren't my mother's or God's. I started to skip school a lot, traveling back and forth to Boston to see a man - well, maybe a few men.

As I approached my junior year at Southeastern Regional Vocational, my life was starting to take more of a nosedive. I would say that I was going to catch my school bus but get to the top of the hill and go in another direction. I didn't care what would happen to me as long as I wasn't at my house.

Considering the kind of life I was leading, I didn't think I would live much longer. The men I knew were ruthless. They didn't care about anything, never mind me. They were drug dealers and pimps equipped with guns.

By the end of my 12th year of high school, I had made it through school without getting into any fighting. Then a month and a half before I was to graduate, I got into a fight. I couldn't even tell you what the fight was over. I was suspended for five days because the teachers said I started the fight.

My mother was not at all happy with the choices I was making. You couldn't blame her. I put my mother through a lot. I was living a fast life and didn't care what anyone thought or said. My attitude then was that I was going to do what I wanted to do. The choices I made, how I felt at home, and feeling so alone formed my life for the years to come.

7. The Man of My Dreams

Before graduating from high school in July of 2001, I had met a man I thought I would be in a long-term relationship with. His name was Ty. Until this point, I felt I was just skidding by in the world, barely making it. Ty made me feel wanted. I was 18 years old, and he was 24.

We started to hang out in Brighton, MA, where he lived. We would go to the movies and out to eat; things were good. He didn't know much about my past, and that's the way I wanted to keep it. After a few months of being together, I discovered I was pregnant with my first son Naseim. Ty was excited, but I think his mother was more excited than he was. My grandmother was very excited that she would be a great-grandmother, and my great-grandmother was also excited.

My mother and stepdad, I call him Dad, sat down with Ty and had a serious talk. It was so humiliating, but it was needed. Everything was going well for a while. Ty moved into my mother's house where we shared a bed. For the first time, I had what I thought was the perfect life.

8. My First Son

On January 17th of 2002, I had my son. He was very small. During the first half of my pregnancy, I was stressed out and had a lot of arguments, which took a toll on my unborn son. Naseim was only 5lbs 8 oz when he was born, and I felt guilty. He had some physical health issues and a learning disability, but he was mine.

Not long after he was born, Ty and I started having problems. He was cheating and staying out all night. I wouldn't see him for at least a day or so. Also, I had to deal with women calling his phone and his friends, who were always wanting him to go to clubs every week.

When I got pregnant, I was 18 and focused on how badly I wanted a boyfriend. I didn't count the cost. By having Naseim, I thought he would be that missing piece in my life, that he would love me, and I would feel so much happier.

I expected my issues to disappear if I had someone to love me. Ty didn't want to help with Naseim. He made every excuse not to, and I soon found out that he was seeing the same woman he was with when I first met him. Looking back, maybe it's what

I deserved. I made an impulse decision yet again instead of thinking through things.

9. My Days of Prostitution

When Naseim turned 1, I met another man who changed my life. He wasn't the man I was hoping to meet, but it happened all the same. He was so good-looking; tall, with brown skin, hazel brown eyes, and muscular. The only problem I had with him, which I didn't figure out until after I grew to care for him, was that he was a pimp. He told me he would love me like no one else could and protect me from all harm. It was the same nonsense I had been hearing from men for a while, but what made him different from the rest was his sex and his body type. He assured me everything would be ok, especially when he called me daily. We would discuss if I did certain things; he would make it worth my while.

I was desperate and needed love, and I wanted to be shown love not just with material things but by someone going out of their way to prove to me how much they loved me. The one thing I didn't think of was that it came with conditions and consequences. I just wanted to be loved, not realizing that so many already loved me.

I got into the prostitution game, and it was so degrading. I couldn't talk to any other black man when I was with him. He controlled me so much that I even had to ask him if I could leave the house. In that world, everything you earn has to be turned over to your pimp. I couldn't even keep a dollar. My family didn't really have a clue, but some questions arose. Guys were going in and out of the house at all times of the night, but that was the life he was in. He didn't see anything wrong with it, and neither did I.

I loved the attention from men, so it was right up my alley. A few months into it, I said something to him that he thought was disrespectful. I can only remember leaning up against the door and being shown a gun. He didn't point it at me but said he would use it if I tried to leave. I wanted someone to love me so badly that I risked my baby's life and mine.

One night, I had one of the biggest scares of my life. I got into a car with a man who told me that he would be my last date. Apparently, he was going to take my life. I didn't know what to say or do after hearing that I wouldn't make it out of his car alive. As we approached a set of lights, the doors to the car unlocked themselves. Now we can make up reasons why the doors unlocked, that there was a malfunction, that every time the car comes to a stop light, the doors unlock. To this day, I think God freed me from that situation. I got out of the car and returned to where I was picked up from.

Despite all the sex I wanted, I felt it was time to reconsider based on what I just experienced. I told my pimp, the man who said he would protect me from things like this, that I couldn't do it anymore. I was done and leaving for good. It was a risk, as everything prostitutes were taught not to do – mainly talking back to their pimps.

I knew that I was not supposed to. I walked past a black man while the man was on the sidewalk, looking directly at him. Everything I knew I should not do while being a prostitute, I did the complete opposite, I was showing the man that was out there with no respect. Maybe I was at my breaking point and just didn't care who I disrespected. I was completely out of pocket, as they say.

As my pimp and I got back to the house, I stormed past everyone sitting in the living room, still not caring about all the rules I was breaking. I had been beaten with a belt before, but to get beat with the buckle was something that I wouldn't wish on my worst enemy. I had cuts going across my arms and legs. I remember falling off the bed, and he picked me up off the floor, slamming my head into the wall four times. He then told me to get in the bed and to take my clothes off, where I lay bruised and beaten while he raped me. I was scared to tell him no, afraid of what he would do. I didn't want him to go anywhere near that closet where the gun was. I didn't realize how bad the lacerations were until the next morning. I had so many. I lay in bed, planning an escape.

10. Finding The Determination To Leave

By 9 am the next day, I had figured out how I would leave and what I would say to this man. However, when I woke up, I realized he had left. He wasn't at the house. My son was in Brighton with his great-grandmother. My abuser being gone allowed me to leave and get my son.

I missed the bus, so I was walking back to the house. Suddenly there was a swarm of Boston police and the F.B.I. I couldn't believe it. I told my mother not to call the police, but she did. I turned back toward the bus stop and walked fast. I made it down to Brighton, where my son was.

My son's great-grandmother saw all the lacerations and didn't know what to say. The police showed up there and asked me questions, wanting to see where this man was. I didn't know. Once the cops left, my son's great-grandmother and father, Ty, humiliated me. They called me names, stared, and sneered.

Ty's family, except for his mother, was trying so hard to get custody of my son Naseim but they failed. Even Ty disagreed with what his family was saying. He didn't want them to take my son because he knew they were only interested in adopting kids for the money they would get from the state.

I couldn't take it, so I called my Aunt Yvette to have her come get me. She was surprised to hear from me, yet she didn't tell me why until she arrived. While in the car with my aunt and her friend Monica, they explained why they were so surprised. It was because when the police searched the home where I was beaten, they found a dead body on the third floor. The police thought it was me because they couldn't find me when they arrived. Hearing that caught me off guard. It was terrifying to hear that they all thought I was dead.

When I came home, my mother was so hurt. She was curled up like a baby. To see her like that caused me pain. After this incident, I moved away from my family briefly.

11. Caretaker and a Loss

At the age of 20, I moved back home. I was getting tired of going from man to man to man and being paid for sex. I wanted to take care of my grandmother, who was very sick. She had surgery and needed someone to care for her needs, like cooking and dispensing her medications. I also had to help with my great-grandmother, and I still had my son to care for.

During this time, I went back to school to further my education. I was able to go to school and help my family, but it wasn't easy. Around Halloween that year, my grandmother's condition worsened. She suffered a stroke, and she never came out of it. She was in the hospital all the way up until she passed away on January 2, 2004. She passed away with her children and grandchildren around her. I never thought I'd see my grandmother take her last breath. The nurses turned off the machine so we would not hear the flatline, but we knew she was gone.

Later that night, we returned home to tell my great-grandmother that her only daughter had passed away. Before we said anything, she already knew. She was so hurt, but she possessed so much wisdom. Experiencing my grandmother's death, preparing for her funeral, taking care of my son, and taking care of my great-grandmother all at once was overwhelming.

During that process, I had to deal with my desires, sex. It felt selfish, but I also thought I couldn't help myself. I tried to mask the pain and make sacrifices to please those around me. Ultimately, I was drowning, ignoring my needs and trying to meet everyone else's needs. I was dying inside. Sex was just a convenient way to attempt to fix what I was missing in my life. It was quick and easy, and I hadn't yet realized it wasn't going to help me. By then, I had already become a sex addict, and taking care of anything else without caring for myself was challenging. I took care of my great-grandmother for almost a year and a half. She was so tired, yet she fought to the very end.

12. Yet Another Devastating Loss

One day, I went to wake my great-grandmother for her morning routine: washing her, brushing her hair, giving her medications, and feeding her breakfast. I called her name, "Ma" but she didn't answer me. I called her a few times, and she didn't answer. As I got closer, I saw she was staring up at the ceiling, not blinking but still breathing. I didn't know what to do, so I got my mother on the phone. I had to call the ambulance for them to come to get her. I didn't want her to leave. I felt like I was doing so well taking care of her and that she needed me. Really, I needed her even more. The ambulance finally got there and took her to the hospital, but soon she had to be transferred to a different hospital that was better equipped to care for her.

She was transferred to a hospital in Boston, Massachusetts, where she passed away on April 18, 2005. With half of the family around her, I saw her take her last breath as I held her hand. Her passing was extremely hard for me. After all, she raised me. She gave up her life for me, my sister, and my cousins. I was still looking for someone to love me, and she always had. She was like my best friend. It may sound selfish that the only person I could think about was myself at this time, knowing my mother, sister, and other family members were also grieving her loss. Addicts don't care about anyone but themselves.

After her passing, my sex needs increased. Sex was the only thing on my mind other than my son. It was hard for me to take care of a child and feed my sexual desires. No one knew how much I struggled with this addiction. I had to have all this sex to make up for all the hurt I felt inside. I was crying out for love and attention. When I wasn't caring for my son, I was with a man.

At this point, I knew a lot of men, whether they were a boyfriend or just friends with benefits. Sometimes I had to do things that didn't make me feel comfortable, but, for example, if I had no way of getting back home, I had to compromise. There were also times I enjoyed what I was doing, letting a man take complete control of my body. I liked to tell them they had total control, which wasn't a good idea because sometimes the role-play went too far. But then, sometimes, I would enjoy how far it would go. I enjoyed being tied up, strangled and hurt. I didn't care how those guys looked at me. I had to drink, to escape the memory of what I did. I didn't want to face my reality. It was hard for me to care about myself.

There were days I felt disgusting and disgraceful, but other days I didn't care. I had no self-respect, and my self-esteem was at an all-time low. No matter how many times someone spoke positively in my life, I could not accept it. I refused to let in anything good. People would ask why I downplayed my looks and didn't feel good about myself. It went back to my upbringing.

Growing up, I could never do anything right; even if I did, it changed quickly, and someone was upset. After hearing all the negativity all my life, why would I believe anything different? My heart and spirit were broken beyond repair. Or so I thought.

13. The Abuse

At the age of 25, I met the man I hoped was going to change my way of thinking. Yet again, I was relying on someone else to change my life. At first, I thought I wouldn't have to have sex with him all the time to please him. Well, I was wrong. Straight away, it was all about the sex. There wasn't one time we got together that it wasn't about sex.

We moved in together, and everything was going great in the beginning. He would buy me clothes, bring things for my son, and take care of us. The only thing I had to do was take care of him. I wasn't sure how to take care of him except by using my body. I was nothing but a piece of meat to this man. I tried to break out of the sex mindset, but that made things worse.

He knew me better than I knew myself. I didn't think I was strong enough to be different, to change. There were times when I wouldn't have sex with him. He would get so mad with me that he would take it. It didn't matter to him if I said no. No, meant yes to him; what I said didn't matter. He had no respect for me as a woman or as the soon-to-be mother of his children. My body was his and no one else's, not even my own. I didn't know how to feel, so I bottle everything inside.

Even aside from the sex, he was a very controlling man. It was what he wanted, how, and when he wanted it.

Looking back, I can say I was crazy for staying with him. This man and I welcomed our first child together, Evyn. I thought this child would change how he looked at me, how I looked at myself, and how others looked at me. Again, I was counting on the void to be filled. Of course, that didn't happen. When I wasn't being a mother to my two children, I was his unwilling sex slave. I wasn't in control; he was. He worked hard to get this through my head by slamming me against doors, embarrassing me, and reminding me that if he couldn't have me, no one would.

I was surprised that I found myself in another abusive relationship with a man I loved. Everything he wanted, I did, and everything he said, I believed. Nobody could tell me anything bad about him without me catching an attitude.

He had brainwashed me. Mentally and emotionally beaten me down to a point where I couldn't even recognize what he was doing and saying was wrong. The moment he slammed me against the door with his hand wrapped around my neck should have been a red flag. But in my mind, that was a way of someone telling me how much they loved me, so I accepted it all.

I gave this man permission. I gave him the key to treat me that way, and he knew that and played on it. The abuse only got worse. There were many trips down to the police station, the courthouse, and restraining orders. In all, I had about seven restraining orders. He violated a couple of orders, but I only called the police once. That time I was slammed against a window, and the windows shattered on my back. He dragged me across the wall in front of my two sons, threatened me with a baseball bat because I wouldn't give him money to buy drugs, and punched me in the face.

When I told my family I was pregnant again, they asked me, "Is he really abusing you?" They couldn't believe a rational woman would stay in an abusive relationship with two children. Their points were valid. A few months into my pregnancy, I got a job in a different city than where I lived. I had to catch a train from Brockton, Massachusetts to Boston, Massachusetts. I would ask for a ride to work, and he didn't help. He would tell me I shouldn't have taken the job in the first place.

One day as my son Evyn and I were getting off the train, I called my boyfriend to pick up Evyn so he didn't have to walk home in the rain. He agreed to get him, and he showed up five minutes later. As I put Evyn into the car seat, he asked me to get into the car. I didn't want to be near him as he was acting weirdly. I decided to start walking home. I took a few steps and heard the engine pick up speed. He would have run me over with the car if I had taken another step, killing me and our unborn daughter. I knew that I had to get him out of my house.

14. He Left Me Broken

One day, when I was about 29 years old, I came home to find his clothes packed. I asked him where he was going. He told me he was leaving, that he was going to live with another woman. It was hard because I was pregnant with my 3rd child, and so broken that I thought I needed him to survive. I depended on him for almost everything.

Shortly after, I had my third child, Evelyn. Her father was not at the hospital for many reasons, but just to be sure, I didn't tell him I had given birth. I wanted that experience to be joyful without complaining, fighting, or fear.

Eventually, I told him that I had Evelyn. He was upset that I kept it from him but happy at the same time and asked me if he could move back in with me and the kids. When I asked him why he said he missed me and had nowhere else to go. Thinking about how he left me for another woman while I was pregnant, I said no.

While we were still together, one day he asked me about a cookout, letting me know I was invited. I had agreed that we would go, so he came by to pick up me and the kids. I had a strange feeling about the whole thing, so when he arrived, I told him I had changed my mind and we weren't going. I knew he would be furious, so I was trying to put my son behind me so he wouldn't take him. This put me in an awkward position by the door. He asked me for the kids again, and I said no. I remember my head hitting the door. My daughter was in my arms when he punched me in the eye, and I almost dropped her. As he moved away from me, I managed to make it to the bassinet before I dropped her. My son was still behind me. I was trying to protect him as I yelled for this man to leave. I went over to the mirror and saw I had a black eye. That image still haunts me to this day. My stepfather came down to where we were because he heard a commotion, and I told my step dad what had happened, but he didn't believe me.

After that day, there were many times the police were involved. The same police repeatedly, the same judge hearing the same story. I got so tired of being inside of that courthouse. I got so tired of being anywhere in the judicial system. The judge was so tired of the nonsense between me and him. I had to face reality. I was told that I should go back with him and call the police again, D.S.S. would have to be involved. They would have said I wasn't protecting my children and would file a 51A on me – a report of child abuse or neglect. This was a pivotal moment for me.

Taking care of three children, dealing with the court system, and dealing with his abuse drove me to drink. If only I had taken the time to learn more about God like my family was telling me so many years ago. If only I had opened myself up to going to church.

Looking back, I know that if I had realized it was God I was searching for, this wouldn't have happened to me. God looked after me the entire time, but I couldn't recognize it back then. I didn't think He cared about a woman like me. I felt no one knew or understood what I was going through, so I was not open to any advice.

One day it was recommended that I talk to a psychologist. I didn't think it was a good idea because they had ways of bringing out the truth. I wasn't ready to face some of my demons, but as I thought more about it and my life became even more depressing, I realized it might be what I needed. I didn't want to carry on with the loss of sleep, not being able to eat, loss of hair, the headaches, and not being the mother I should have been to my children because I lowered my standards.

I went to the psychologist, and I was asked so many questions. She was concerned with my state of mind but more concerned about my children. I wasn't working, had just gotten out of an abusive relationship, was going to school part-time with three children, and drank. This therapist showed me mercy, she could have very well called the police on me that day, but she gave me a chance to get things in order. I was given a prescription drug for depression and insomnia. I got back to my house and threw out every liquor bottle. I wouldn't compromise my children's or my lives any longer.

15. The Woman: Abomination

At the age of 35, I became sexually involved with a woman. I felt it was wrong not because of religion but because I was always taught that it was disgusting to lie down with the same sex. Also, I had to sneak around to see her and lie about who I was talking to for hours at a time. Getting involved with her was easier than getting out of the relationship. Once again, I was caught up in having sex. Every time I was with her, I couldn't say no. She would come out every weekend, and we would stay in the house most days and have sex.

One night as I was coming back from dropping off my lover. My daughter and I were in my car, and I was on RT 146 in North Smithfield, Rhode Island. I must have fallen asleep at the wheel. When I opened my eyes, I soon realized I was going at least 55 miles per hour toward a broken-down 18-wheeler in front of me. I felt God telling me to wake up, in a literal sense and spiritual sense. That scared me. I had been going to church by this point but didn't know much about Him. You would think I would have seen this as a sign to stop seeing this woman, but I didn't.

One of the few reasons why I stopped seeing her was because of a fight I had with my mother. My kids were there at the apartment to witness it. My kids didn't need to hear or see what was happening. They already had seen and heard enough.

My Pastor also spoke to me daily, warning me of my choices. The choice I was making started to impact my life. I was having dreams of sex with women, dreams of sex with multiple women. The thoughts haunted me for a while. The dreams were horrible. They were almost like nightmares that I could not escape from.

I started to cry out to the Lord Jesus for help. Yes, the same Lord I wanted nothing to do with, the one I didn't think would help me, the one I didn't think wanted a woman like me. At this point, I didn't really know Jesus, but I knew I could call on Him when I was fighting a battle I couldn't handle alone. "For we wrestle not against flesh and blood but against principalities, against powers, against the rulers of the darkness of the world, against spiritual wickedness in high places" (Ephesians 6:12). I had to cry out to the Lord for many things that had come my way.

My sex addiction, I knew I had a problem but was trying to suppress it. The Lord tells us to "Cast all your anxiety on him because he cares for us" (Peter 5:7). I had a hard time doing that because I felt ashamed of my sin. What I failed to realize was that God already knew. He just wanted me to open my mouth and talk to him. He met me right where I was. I was expecting one thing, but I got something different from The Lord, a love I can't explain.

16. After Jesus Christ

In November 2018, I did the right thing and was baptized. I didn't know much about Jesus but was willing to learn everything I could about Him and all He did for me at Calvary. The one thing that caught me off guard was being a target for the enemy because of my choice to follow the spiritual path of God.

The Minister of the church was my mentor. She told me because of my decision, the enemy would be on my tail, and boy, was she right. She also said that a lot of people would not agree with me. We must make many choices to be a follower of Christ. I had so many people coming at me. I was told I should have waited for people to be there at my baptism, but I waited too long as it was. Don't people know tomorrow is not promised? That the Lord can call you at any time? Once God says times up, He means times up. Too many things were happening to me to keep waiting and putting it off. I realized I was playing Russian roulette with my life. I was knocking on hell's door, and I was in desperate need of a Savior.

Even then, I still wanted to keep my life the way it was. I loved men, and I loved having sex, but I felt my lifestyle was going to cost me in the end if I didn't choose God. I would burn in hell for eternity if I didn't repent and ask the Lord for forgiveness.

To be honest, I thought everything would change when I came out of the water, but I still had the same attitude. Although, at the same time, I felt a difference. I felt lighter. I felt weak- like I couldn't stand up. I was in someone's arms, stepping off the ladder. She cared for me and stayed with me the entire time while another Minister cared for my daughter.

It was hard for me to acknowledge that I, a fornicator and a sinner, once a 16-year-old who said God couldn't change her, a woman so far gone who wanted nothing to do with God, had finally given her life to Jesus.

17. God Saves My Life Again

I was on 95 a few weeks later, traveling home from a revival. Four cars were in front of me; three of them had hit a dead deer. Unfortunately, I was one of them that hit it while I was going at least 70mph. I thought my car was going to flip. I had to pull over, and the car started to smoke once I did. It smelled horrible. Myself and three other motorists called the fire department to ensure that our cars didn't catch fire.

Shortly after they arrived, the fire department said I could drive my car. A few cars that hit the deer first had to be towed. God protected me because it could have gone in a completely different direction. Glory to God! I made it home thirty minutes later. I thought my car was fine and had nothing to worry about. After calming down, I went to sleep that night, thinking about what had happened. I woke up the next morning and found my right front tire flat. I turned my car on for the tow company to pick it up, and the deer smell filled the air. It was horrible, but I thank God that only a tire went flat, and my life was spared. Again, because I decided to give my life to Christ, I still had this Spirit that would not leave me alone.

Through my sex addiction, I was a slave of Satan. I was disgusted by those thoughts of being his slave. I didn't return to my female partner, and although she didn't stop calling me, I never responded. I had to use all that was in me to resist the enemy. The Bible says, "Submit yourselves, then, to God. Resist the devil, and he will flee from you" (James 4:7). She eventually stopped texting and calling me after a couple of months.

Once, I told a few men that I had turned my life to Jesus. Many people said I made a bad decision and that it wasn't who I was, but I kept going and didn't pay them any mind. The enemy was using them to get to me. They thought they knew me. I knew my background and the things I survived, but I didn't consider the things I had to contend with in the days ahead.

I attended church every Sunday, bible study, and the new convert class at Pentecostal of Boston. I would faithfully attend church twice a week; rain and snow, I was there.

18. The Struggle

In 2019, I was still dealing with life's challenges and trying to escape from the things I got myself into before being saved. The sin of sexual perversion was so heavy on me, so I prayed and asked people to pray for me, but I never told them why they were praying for me. I was just too embarrassed to say anything. I even had a hard time being honest with myself. I struggled with who I was and still struggle with my identity.

There was and still is a battle going on in my own mind. Even though I was Saved, I still had people who reminded me of my past; how many men I slept with, the woman I slept with, selling my body to make money. I struggled with the desire to return to that life, but luckily an even bigger part of me knew I couldn't. I had come too far.

There were some things I had to deal with, but I didn't want to tell God, even though He already knew. I didn't want to be honest with Him and say, "God, I need more of you. I am struggling with who I am. I am struggling because no one in my family takes me seriously." I was trying to change, but I kept being reminded of the past that I was trying to forget. I felt the Lord telling me, "You are no longer that person."

19. The Temptations

I didn't know much but knew I was sinking with my head just a little above water. I still had guys calling me, and I didn't decline their calls. Sometimes, I would answer them and deliberately talk about the past.

In the past, I wanted to be a slave to a man. I did anything to make them happy as long as they pleased me. I was no longer that person. Still having the same men reaching out to me, it was tough to turn away and not answer their messages. Resisting the temptations of having sex anytime I wanted, with no strings attached, was hard. I only had God to answer to.

20. Covid-19

In 2020 the Covid-19 pandemic happened. Seeing people dying from this virus, people hospitalized, being put on ventilators, losing limbs, and having to go on dialysis was very disturbing. I even lost a friend from Covid-19 complications that year. It was so hard because she was in a rehab facility when she caught it. She had no way to fight it off. We prayed for her strength and peace and that the Lord would bring her up and out of that place. She will be walking soon. Once, I was invited onto a prayer line to stand in the gap and pray for a sister-in-Christ's family member. She was on a ventilator, and we were unsure if she would make it. But Glory to be God, she did pull through. I had never prayed for healing so much before in my life. I never prayed as much about something as I did for people's deliverance from Covid. I couldn't imagine how it would affect me personally.

I came down with Covid-19 in the first week of September 2020. I had a hard time breathing, a terrible cough, and a fever, so I had to call the ambulance. That's when they told me I had Covid. I couldn't believe I had this virus. Where did I get it from? The only thing that went through my mind was fear of my death and my children. Who was going to take care of them? I also wondered if I had time to get my affairs in order. A couple of hours after being diagnosed at the hospital, they felt that I was healthy enough to go home. There was no one to come get me, so I walked home.

It was just me and God on that walk. I told God, "Your Will be done. I don't know what it will be, but whatever it is, Father, your Will be done." I finally made it home after half an hour of walking. Once I made it upstairs to my bed, I collapsed. I was so tired and sick.

During this time, I dreamt of what it was like being in hell. God showed me how I needed to change. I was sick for a few weeks. My family knew that I had Covid, but no one would take my kids to make sure they wouldn't catch it. My kids were right next to me, through the fever and everything. By God's grace, my children never caught it. My son Evyn prayed for me and cried, asking when I would get better. I didn't have an answer for him, but God knew. I had to push myself. I had to call on the saints and ask the pastors and ministers to pray for me. I needed the body of Christ to intercede for my healing.

I'm so grateful that this virus didn't have long-lasting effects. After a few weeks, I was finally starting to regain my strength, and my health was beginning to improve. One day, I felt pain when I was breathing, so I went to the hospital. I had never experienced that kind of pain, and I feared it was part of the

Covid nightmare I had experienced. The hospital ran tests on me, and what they found had nothing to do with Covid. I praised God for that. I know it could have been much worse. I could have been on a ventilator, in a hospital bed, but God turned it all around for me. He gets the Glory out of my life. He delivered me from the virus.

I often wonder, did I go through what I went through because of my disobedience or because I wasn't listening to God's instructions? I didn't want to ever go through that again, so I followed God's plan and did what I could. I slipped up once in a while because I'm only human, but I had to repent of my sins, the disobedience, thoughts, and decisions I made that were not pleasing to God. I had to keep fighting, knowing that if I didn't give up on God, God wouldn't give up on me.

It was hard to hear people asking me where God was when I had Covid-19. It was difficult hearing them say that God didn't care about me, God wasn't there for me when I was sick. It hurt my feelings badly, knowing how much I knew God was with me the entire time and then to hear someone speak contrary to what I believed. I moved past it because I know God is a healer, a promise keeper, and a present help in times of trouble. As long as I keep looking to the hills, I know that He will come through for me and take care of me and my children. He is the author and finisher of my Faith. After my fight with Covid, I knew he wasn't done with me.

21. The Loss of My Sister Chanel

In 2021, I would face another life-altering change, a change I didn't want and didn't see coming. My sister Chanel was my protector here on earth. She didn't allow anyone to bother me or mess with me. She pushed me to start my non-profit, The Becoming, and to start a cooking business. God truly blessed her with the knowledge to work with computers and speak eloquently. She was so intelligent, putting spreadsheets together, doing my flyers up when I was giving away food to people experiencing homelessness, and creating my website for The Becoming. She was very strong and courageous in all she did. God blessed me with an amazing sister, my big sister C.T., The Diva.

In August 2021, my sister Chanel went into the hospital for the final time when she was diagnosed with Covid. She was also very sick from diabetes. A year prior, she had a few toes amputated. I cared for her needs, taking her to the clinic, changing her bandages, etc. When she contracted Covid, she was in the hospital for about a month with a lot of uncertainty regarding her brain. They didn't know much damage had been done until she came out from sedation.

One night in a dream, I saw Chanel sitting at the edge of a hospital bed with two women on each side of her. The scenery was all white. They asked her, "Chanel, are you ready to go?" Chanel answered, "Yes, I'm ready." I didn't quite understand what she meant by "ready," but I eventually got my answer.

I had to pray and keep praying. I asked for prayers from the members of the groups I was in and the churches I was involved with. I knew God was going to heal her. I didn't know how he was going to do it. I prayed and asked the Lord to give Chanel another chance at salvation and send her back to me. That prayer was prayed toward the middle of August, and God sent Chanel back to me for a few days. Glory to God!

On September 5th and 6th, I spent time with her. I prayed over her, and we listened to her favorite songs. She would follow me all around the room as far as the cord would allow her to go. She squeezed my hands when I asked her to. It was beautiful.

On September 7th, I had planned on going up there at noon but was told not to because Chanel's blood pressure was unstable, and she was very sick. That day the hospital was in contact with my mother and me more than any day before. They had planned on removing the tubes from her throat. Things were supposedly moving in the right direction. I left the house to pick up my mother to get lunch. About five minutes from the restaurant, I pulled over to the side of the road and called two of my aunts, and asked them to pray with me for Chanel, and they agreed.

The prayer was that God would have His way, for His Will to be done regarding Chanel. I knew that once I said for Him to have His way, something would happen.

About twenty minutes later, I got a call from an unknown number. Unfortunately, my phone died before I had a chance to answer. My mother got a call from what I found out was the same number. A doctor was calling to tell us that we needed to get to the hospital as quickly as possible, Chanel was not going to make it.

My mother went crazy. I wanted to stay but had to try to make it to Chanel. I grabbed my mother's car keys, my pocketbook, and my cell phone. Once I got in the car, I asked God to help me and let me make it there to see her so she wouldn't die alone. I managed to charge my cell phone, and the same number called me again as I was ten minutes from the hospital. This time it was the doctor telling me Chanel had passed away. He apologized over and over again, but there was nothing he could say that was going to take away the pain of losing my only sister. The doctor told me to still come and view her body.

I finally reached the hospital and felt numb, still calling on Jesus. I didn't know what else to do or who to call on but Jesus. I made it to Chanel's floor, and the doctor met me at the elevator. They explained what they thought could have happened. I asked them if Chanel struggled to breathe, and they said they believed she did, so I broke down and cried. The doctors would not allow me to enter the room until I calmed down. I told them I was ok, and they gave me a cup of water and a box of tissues before seeing her.

A doctor walked me into the room, pulled back the closed curtain, and there I saw my big sister's lifeless body. I then knew that in my dream, when she said she was ready, she meant she was ready to go home with the Lord, to be with Him who loved her so much. She searched for Him to love her while on earth, to show her the love she had always wanted from our earthly father, which he didn't give her.

22. The Presence

It felt like I was in a nightmare, like it wasn't real. I asked myself, "Was I really seeing this? Was I really experiencing this? How was I going to go on without her? Why did this happen to her, of all people?" So many different thoughts consumed my mind. I couldn't grasp that she would no longer squeeze my arm, help me watch my children, be mad with me over the least little thing, go to the flea markets with me, or be there for me, period. I was standing at the end of her hospital bed, and the presence in the room was indescribable. It was peace, but also it was movement. It was as if someone was standing next to me. I stayed there with her for an hour or so, asking myself what happened. My heart was broken, shattered into pieces.

God was there with me in that room. It was an amazing feeling. The almighty God never left my side for one moment. He gave me strength at the right time and at the right place.

23. Facing reality

I finally left the hospital. It hurt because I knew that was my last time going up there to see her. She was no longer there, just her shell. The hardest part I had to do was go back home, see my mother, and tell my daughter that her best friend - Auntie Chanel - had gone to be with the Lord. Trying to break it down to a 9-year-old was tough, but my children knew God. I explained that He is a spirit, which means Chanel is also a spirit. Oh, how I miss her every day. If it weren't for God, where would I be? Where would my mind be? God kept my sanity, saved me from going off the deep end, and kept me from returning to my past. He kept me so I wouldn't let go.

24. God Supplies ALL of My Needs

Since Chanel's death, my family has turned their back on me. They didn't even call to see how I was doing. But God has been there since Chanel left her earthly shell until now. In 2021 my children and I experienced homelessness, and we had to stay in a hotel for about three weeks. I didn't know how the room would get paid, but God ensured everything was covered. He supplied all our needs, opened doors for my children, blessed me with a job, and blessed me with people I needed then. God knew exactly what I needed even before I asked him. A church in Louisiana paid a week for us to be there. It was a blessing from God. Everything was. I can never doubt God's moves, faithfulness, and love. He is an amazing Father that loves His children. I'm incredibly blessed to be a child of the highest God. God delivered me once again.

25. The Move

In December 2021, I left the hotel and moved to Indiana with a sister-in-Christ and her two children. My sister-in-Christ has undoubtedly supported me, especially in prayer. My friend blessed me and paid for my children and me to travel to Indiana.

God was with me the entire time, healing, restoring, and strengthening me. He gave me all that I needed that season. He was and is still here with me, whether it's through peace, strength, healing, direction, or restoration.

It was a nice change in my scenery. While traveling on the Greyhound bus, I could sit back, relax and enjoy the ride. Even though I was still struggling with the loss of my sister, being around people other than my family was soothing, and so much peace and no drama.

While in Indiana, I could think clearly and not worry about how bills would get paid. I learned a few revelations about myself that I did not know. For example, I learned how to lean more on God. Also, I could do many things, including taking care of my children and myself, without the help of my family. The same ones that told me that I wouldn't make it with them or I couldn't maintain my life without their help.

I was so happy to be away but missed my oldest son, Naseim; he didn't want to come with me. During my time away, my grandmother passed away from Covid-19 complications; I did not find out she was in the hospital until she had passed away. So I did not have a chance to attend her funeral, say I loved her, or say goodbye because my family craved control.

On August 28, 2022, I returned home to Rhode Island. It was not easy leaving. I learned how to be independent while in Indiana and learned how to take care of my children and myself. I had so much peace in Indiana, but my time there had ended.

Returning home to Rhode Island was difficult after eight months of being away. I didn't know how my return was going to be since the passing of my sister Chanel. Life had its challenges, especially with my daughter no longer seeing her best friend. I was used to Chanel coming by the house, causing trouble, and being a big sister and an aunt to my children.

God has kept me and is keeping me. The one thing I will say repeatedly about God is that He is a keeper. God has kept His promises. He is faithful. He is a God of justice, love, and compassion. He is a God full of mercy.

26. Reviving

Since I've been back in Rhode Island, I have been able to get myself together. I learned a lot about myself that I never knew, such as what God saw in me that I didn't see in myself and that God was bringing everything I needed in this season to my attention. I am so grateful that I didn't give up when I felt like throwing in the towel because of how people treated me and the lies against me.

My life is finally making sense. I'm finally starting to see that God was the only one I needed this whole time. I made mistakes by putting people in God's place. Yes, I make mistakes and fall short of God's Glory, but He gave me a chance to repent and turn back to Him. The one thing about God is that He won't hold it against you. When everything else failed and fell around me, I had to stand on the rock much higher than I, stand in Faith, and not be moved. God is so amazing in all He does. He can't lie. His love is amazing, and His grace is amazing. Glory to God!

I had to go through the fire to come out on the other side. The Lord is still fine-tuning things inside of me. There is still a lot of life left in me. God is not done with me yet. I cannot be scared or timid of what's to come because it will teach me something about myself and the people around me and more about God and his mercy and grace. I'm truly excited to see what lies in wait for my children and me.

27. God Is Not Done With Me

Again, the Lord is still working on me and working some things out of me, such as my attitude, choices, and the people I associate myself with. I am learning to be solely dependent on Him and Him alone. If we allow it to happen, anything can get into our minds through our eyes and ears.

As the days go by, I'm learning more about myself that I never knew. Maybe I always knew them, but people came into my life and blinded me from the truth and the path God had for me. I'm learning to be a better person, a better mom, a better friend, and a better daughter.

Nothing happens overnight. Everything takes time. It's a gradual process. I'm learning to depend on God even when it doesn't make sense, even when I want to do things my way. I am learning to hear His voice and block out every other voice in my head. The Lord is keeping me grounded in Him instead of doing things that can cause me to regress and get distracted from what He has called me to be. He will allow me to only go so far, stop me in my tracks, and make me ask myself what I'm doing. I want to do all that pleases the Lord.

Sometimes my flesh gets in the way so much. My feelings and my emotions get in the way. If I truly want to be a follower of

Christ, I must live life His way. There are no "but" or "what if". It's either His way or my way but my way will only lead me to destruction.

I have a purpose, I am worthy, I am loved, and I am fearfully and wonderfully made. I am the daughter of Zion. All He asks me to do is believe and trust Him. He will fight my battles.

I'm still going through changes, but the change is good. Nothing is too hard for Jesus; nothing is out of his reach, He fears no man, He is the creator of heaven and earth. Jesus wants our hearts and our attention to be set on him. He knows the problems of this world, and He doesn't want us to be consumed by any of them. My latter days are better than the days behind me. Greater is on the way!

28. God's Promises To His Children

In my life, I had to make some real hard choices, like leaving a home that felt like I was still living in a prison. I had to make the choice to remove myself and my children to a better place in order for me to be free, physically. When I chose to leave after my sister passed away and an argument broke out, I knew it was my time to finally break free and leave everything. I had to trust the Lord would make a way for me. He provided a way of an escape for me and my children.

He provided a roof, a bed and food. He was right there with me. Just when you think that the Lord has left you, that's when He is right there, watching every move you make. He never left me. He stayed true and faithful to my children and I. "It is the Lord who goes before you. He will be with you; he will not leave you or forsake you. Do not fear or be dismayed" (Deuteronomy 31:6-8).

On some days, I felt as if I couldn't do and say anything because of my speech. I stuttered like Moses, was quiet and shy. I kept telling myself I can't, I can't, I can't. But one day after this verse, it clicked months after. That I didn't have to keep saying what I can't do, that I can do it, I can do anything that God will give me the strength to do. "I can do all things through Christ, which strengthened me (Philippians 4:13)".

The Lord is still writing my life, He is still taking things out and putting things in. Rearranging the pieces of my life to fit in His master plan. Jesus died for my sin so I may live a free life. He took my place at the cross, where I should have been. But I am so grateful that He paid the price for me, a price I couldn't pray on my own. "Looking unto Jesus, the author and finisher of our Faith, who for the joy that was set before Him endured the cross, despising the shame, and has sat down at the right hand of the throne of God" (Hebrew 12:2).

29. Jesus Still Loved Me

Even though I was a fornicator, an adulterer in a same-sex relationship, and a prostitute, even though I refused to be accountable for my actions, put people before Him, rejected God, and denied God's power, He has delivered me from it all.

If you are not Saved and haven't given your life to Christ, I pray that reading my story will change your decision. Know that God loves you. I pray that my story was an open opener, an encouragement, and a blessing.

"The Lord is not slack concerning His promise, as some count slackness, but is longsuffering toward us, not willing that any should perish but that all should come to repentance" (2 Peter 3:9).

If you are struggling, my advice is don't stop moving. Don't give up. Turn to Jesus and keep pressing. God will not give up on you, so please don't give up on God. He is with you no matter what you go through in this life. God is a deliverer. If He delivered me, I am sure He can deliver you. There is no one like Him on this earth. He wants to heal you and, most importantly, save, deliver, and set you free.

I'm going to keep going no matter what happens to me or around me. I can't stop now, I've come too far to stop or turn back. It would be a waste if I got all of the wisdom, knowledge and understanding just to resort back to my old ways of life. My prize is found in Jesus. "I press toward the mark for the prize of the high calling of God in Christ Jesus" (Philippians 3:14 K.J.V.).

ABOUT THE AUTHOR

My name is Jade Thomas. I am a mother of three children Naseim, Evyn, and Evelyn. Currently, I am pursuing my Bachelor of Science in Psychology to help and support people, especially children through their problems. I am from Boston, Massachusetts, now living in Rhode Island.

I never thought this day would happen that I would write a book about my life, which is extremely dark because of the domestic violence and alcohol, and prostitution I had endured.

"God Delivered Me from Myself" is dedicated to every woman with the same experiences as me. I want you to know that you can and will make it.

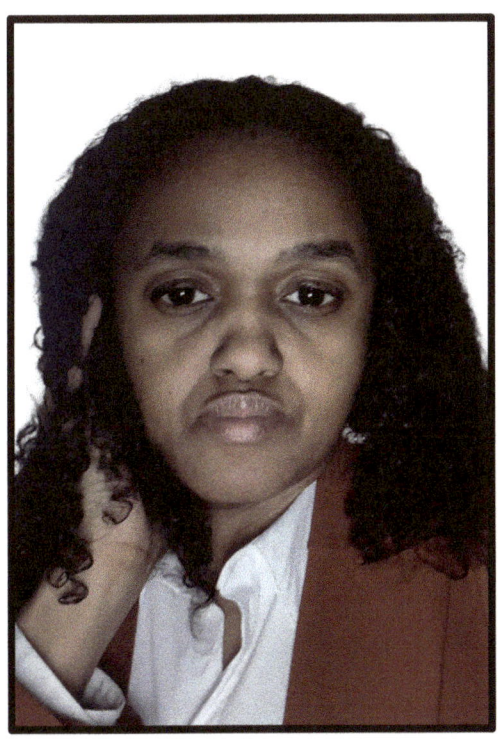

www.ingramcontent.com/pod-product-compliance
Lightning Source LLC
LaVergne TN
LVHW061626070526
838199LV00070B/6590